Confidence

How to Overcome Your Limiting Beliefs and Achieve Your Goals

By Martin Meadows

Download another Book for Free

I want to thank you for buying my book and offer you another book (almost two times longer than this book), *Grit: How to Keep Going When You Want to Give Up*, completely free.

Click the link below to receive it:

http://www.profoundselfimprovement.com/selfefficacy

In *Grit*, I'll share with you how exactly to stick to your goals according to peak performers and science.

In addition to getting *Grit*, you'll also have an opportunity to get my new books for free, enter giveaways and receive other valuable emails from me.

Again, here's the link to sign up and get the book:

http://www.profoundselfimprovement.com/selfefficacy

Table of Contents

Download another Book for Free 2

Table of Contents 3

Prologue 5

Chapter 1: What Is Self-Efficacy? 7

Chapter 2: The Experience of Mastery 19

Chapter 3: Social Modeling 31

Chapter 4: Social Persuasion
and Psychological Responses 39

Chapter 5: Five Rules to Develop
a Strong Sense of Self-Efficacy 48

Epilogue 64

Download another Book for Free 67

Could You Help? 68

About Martin Meadows 69

Prologue

Nobody doubts that setting goals is one of the most important keys to making life changes, regardless of whether they're big, audacious goals, or just small adjustments.

Yet, while most of us have no problems identifying goals we want to accomplish, putting these plans into action is frequently much more difficult than we think.

A lack of self-discipline and motivation contribute to this behavior. However, there's another lesser-known reason why some people struggle to make changes in their lives.

It's their low self-efficacy.

Individuals who don't possess much self-efficacy have a hard time putting their plans into action and following through because deep down they don't believe they can achieve them.

You don't even have to be aware you exhibit behavior common among people with low self-efficacy, yet it can dramatically affect your life.

What are the main four factors that affect your self-efficacy? How can you develop more confidence in your abilities? What are the most important things you need to know about the influence of your mind on your achievements?

These are some of the questions I'll answer in this short book. The advice you're about to read is based both on scientific research and my personal experience.

Instead of delving deep into the details, I will share fundamental knowledge that will make the most difference in your life.

My goal is to help you understand how to develop more confidence in your abilities and avoid the most common dangers associated with low self-efficacy.

Let's start with explaining in more detail what self-efficacy is.

Chapter 1: What Is Self-Efficacy?

Self-efficacy is the strength of your beliefs in your ability to complete tasks successfully. It determines things such as:

- whether you will persist or give up while working on a specific task,

- how long you will stick to uncomfortable changes designed to bring long-term results (diet, workout regimen),

- what goals you'll set for yourself and where "extremely difficult" ends and "impossible" starts.

The beliefs you have about your abilities shape your entire life. They affect how you think, feel, and behave[i]. If you have little self-efficacy, you'll have a tendency to write off things you consider impossible. As a result, for the sole reason you don't believe you're able to achieve your dreams you'll live a mediocre life instead of realizing your full potential.

It's important to note that self-efficacy is task-related. You can have high self-efficacy when driving a car and low self-efficacy when working on your business.

However, high self-efficacy in specific tasks indirectly translates to higher self-efficacy in other areas (for the reason we'll discuss in the second chapter). In other words, high self-efficacy in one area will help you start with the right mindset in another area of your life.

You Can Improve Your Self-Efficacy Even as an Adult

General self-efficacy develops during childhood. The right teacher can help her students develop a powerful belief in their abilities that will empower them in their adult life.

However, nothing is lost for the rest of the people who haven't developed a strong sense of self-efficacy when they were young.

There are ways to develop self-efficacy as an adult, and that's what we're going to focus on in this book. Put away the past and let's focus on what we can do about it now.

People with a Strong Sense of Self-Efficacy vs. People with a Weak Sense of Self-Efficacy

Here are five common characteristics of people with a strong sense of self-efficacy:

1. They consider challenges as something they can overcome and master.

2. They persevere in the face of difficulties. Obstacles don't make them lose confidence in their abilities.

3. They take responsibility for their failures and believe they control the outcome (i.e., they don't believe in getting lucky).

4. They put more effort into completing a task, which in turn makes them more likely to achieve it.

5. They commit to their goals and develop a deeper understanding of how to achieve them.

And here are five common characteristics of people with a weak sense of self-efficacy:

1. They avoid challenges. Consequently, they rarely (if ever) grow.

2. They believe that difficult goals are beyond their capabilities, and thus they don't set them, and don't achieve big wins.

3. They quickly lose confidence in their abilities and give up on their goals.

4. They tend to take a narrow view of the task and focus on the surface instead of the underlying principles.

5. They don't believe that their actions and decisions make a difference in their life (instead, they believe in external factors like luck).

When I was a shy person with low self-efficacy, I avoided every situation that might have been uncomfortable. My self-confidence soared only when I decided to challenge myself.

These small challenges added up to small wins, which led to big wins. By breaking one behavior that prevented me from developing confidence in my abilities, I've changed my life.

How Self-Efficacy Affects Your Life

The Galatea effect[ii] is a type of a self-fulfilling prophecy that makes our self-expectations largely determine our performance. As a result, low self-efficacy can dramatically lower your chances of achieving personal success.

If you don't believe in your abilities, you aren't likely to set big goals that have the highest chance of making a dramatic improvement in your life. Since you also doubt in your ability to achieve success, you won't do your best (why invest effort in something that's not going to work out, anyway?). On the other hand, if you possess a strong sense of self-efficacy, you constantly set the bar higher and higher and improve yourself on a daily basis.

One area where it's easy to notice this phenomenon is in your career. People who don't believe in their abilities (even if they possess unique and valuable skills) are less likely to apply for better-paid jobs and develop their career.

A small business owner who believes her bakery is the pinnacle of her career won't develop a chain of bakeries, even if she's given an opportunity to do so. Her beliefs will either prevent her from taking action at all, or they will sabotage her later on.

Aside from achievement, the influence of self-efficacy is most visible when you're making health-related decisions[iii].

Your self-efficacy can affect if you're going to keep smoking or quit, start exercising three times per week or live a sedentary lifestyle, or eat healthy or wolf down junk food. In fact, increasing your self-efficacy is one of the best ways to help you stick to your workout regimen[iv].

Since people with low self-efficacy think that many goals are outside their reach, they may never come around to stop smoking. And if they decide to make a change, a low level of self-efficacy will result in expending little effort and little to no perseverance when faced with obstacles.

A person with high self-efficacy will set a goal to stop smoking altogether (and stick to it in the face of difficulties), while a person with low self-efficacy will set a goal to reduce her smoking (and give up when faced with the temptation to smoke more).

The reason why many people struggle to lose weight might be related to their weak sense of self-efficacy, and not just their self-discipline.

Since each failure further decreases your level of self-efficacy (the belief that you can lose weight), you enter a vicious cycle that leads you to even more failure. Soon, you give up your goal to lose weight altogether (because your mind is fixed that you can't achieve it).

Yet, it's still as achievable as it was before, but you perceive it from a self-limiting point of view that puts it in the category of the things impossible to achieve.

Self-Efficacy Is Not Self-Esteem

The chief difference between self-efficacy and self-esteem is that self-efficacy is the belief in your abilities, while self-esteem is the belief in your own worth.

When you have strong self-efficacy, you believe you can achieve certain goals. When you have high self-esteem, you consider yourself a valuable human being – but it doesn't have to affect your self-efficacy, as you can still doubt your abilities.

For instance, a person who's a poor driver would probably have a poor self-efficacy with regard to driving. However, if she doesn't rely on her driving skills as a source of her self-worth, it won't affect her self-esteem.

On the other hand, a person with low self-esteem is more likely to have low self-efficacy because issues with self-esteem usually come with a lack of confidence in general.

If you lack self-confidence, learning new skills is difficult. Moreover, even if you're good at something, your lack of self-worth might make you think you're still inferior to others.

High Self-Efficacy Isn't About Cockiness

Self-efficacy is a good thing as long as you don't mistake it with cockiness. People with a strong sense of self-efficacy are able to meet challenges head on, but it doesn't mean they take on challenges way outside their abilities and expect to achieve success.

Shoshin is a concept of Zen Buddhists meaning "beginner's mind," used mostly when studying Japanese martial arts and Zen Buddhism. It refers to approaching a subject you're studying as a beginner – even when you're already an expert. It's about an open mind, eagerness and a lack of assumptions.

This approach will help you stay humble and, at the same time, keep your mind open to the new opportunities to grow. As Shunryū Suzuki, a Zen Buddhist renowned for founding the first Buddhist monastery outside Asia, said, "In the beginner's mind there are many possibilities, in the expert's mind there are few.[v]"

Don't limit yourself by assuming you know everything.

Four Factors Affecting Self-Efficacy

Psychologist Albert Bandura has identified four factors affecting self-efficacy (listed in the order of importance):

1. Mastery experiences. Success increases self-efficacy, while failure lowers it.

15

2. Social modeling. When you see someone succeeding, your self-efficacy increases. When you see someone fail, your self-efficacy decreases.

3. Social persuasion. Encouragement increases your self-efficacy, while discouragement lowers it.

4. Psychological responses. Experiencing stress can decrease your self-efficacy if you consider it a sign of your inability.

In the next chapters, we'll discuss in more detail each of these factors. I'll also share with you advice on how to handle these sources to develop more self-efficacy.

WHAT IS SELF EFFICACY? QUICK RECAP

1. Self-efficacy determines how strongly you believe in your abilities. It's task-related, which means you can have high self-efficacy in one area and low self-efficacy in another. However, the general sense of self-efficacy affects all aspects of your life, as previous success builds more confidence in your abilities.

2. People with a strong sense of self-efficacy approach challenging tasks as things they can master. They understand that setbacks don't have to lead them to failure, and they put more effort and dedication to achieve their goals.

3. People with a weak sense of self-efficacy avoid challenges and rarely commit to their goals. Consequently, they have a much harder time making changes in their lives.

4. Self-efficacy is not self-esteem. People with a high sense of self-esteem can still suffer from low self-efficacy. However, people with low self-esteem

are more likely to have low self-efficacy due to their general lack of confidence.

5. Self-efficacy isn't about cockiness. Stay humble even when you're good at something. Adapt the approach of a beginner who's open and eager to learn new things without having any preconceptions about the subject she's studying.

6. There are four factors that influence your self-efficacy (listed in the order of importance): mastery experiences, social modeling, social persuasion and psychological responses.

Chapter 2: The Experience of Mastery

The most important factor that influences your self-efficacy is the experience of mastery. When you complete a task successfully, your self-efficacy increases. On the other hand, failure to achieve a goal (or performing inadequately) can undermine and weaken your self-efficacy – especially if you don't believe in your abilities.

As the proverb says, nothing succeeds like success.

If you have ever wondered why successful people are more likely to achieve big goals, here's your answer: success by success, they have built powerful self-efficacy that allows them to believe they can achieve even bigger things.

Although your past performance is the most important factor that influences your self-efficacy, it doesn't mean that if you've experienced a string of failures in the past, you're bound to repeat them. The key to leveraging this source of self-efficacy is to ensure small wins.

Small Wins Lead to Universities in Space

Entrepreneur Peter Diamandis, author of *Bold: How to Go Big, Create Wealth and Impact the World*[vi] emphasizes in his book the power of establishing a track record to achieve big goals.

In 1982, Diamandis came up with an idea to establish an International Space University (yes, a university in space – talk about bold goals). Obviously, the first thing he did wasn't building the university and sending it into space. He broke down his goal into five phases:

1. Organizing a conference about the idea of the International Space University (ISU).

2. Holding a nine-week summer session of the ISU.

3. Repeating the same summer program in countries all over the world to prove the concept works.

4. Establishing a permanent campus on Earth.

5. Establishing a university on the International Space Station.

In 1994, twelve years after setting this big goal, the International Space University established its campus in Strasbourg, France. Diamandis' goal to establish the space university no longer sounds improbable.

His approach is exactly what you need to increase your self-efficacy. While your end goal doesn't have to be as big as his (But why not? We could use more visionaries), the process is exactly the same.

Here's how you can build your self-efficacy to ensure success in building your business:

1. Find your first client in your circle of friends and family. Even if it's your mom, it's still your first client and a necessary step toward gaining self-efficacy to grow a full-blown business.

2. Sell your product to the first stranger. This will give you a powerful boost of motivation that somebody else besides your family and friends is interested in your product.

3. Sell your product to ten strangers. If ten people bought your product, there have to be many more prospects. You're solidifying the belief in your ability to sell.

4. Establish a company and set small sales targets.

5. Hire your first employee.

…

10. Sell on Mars. Or stay on Earth and retire after selling your business for millions of dollars.

And here's how you can build your self-efficacy if all your previous efforts to lose weight failed:

1. Start tracking your calories. It's a simple keystone habit[vii] that will increase your awareness and generate results with little to no resistance.

2. Make a small change to your diet. Eliminate just one high-calorie food that contributes to your unhealthy diet the most. If you successfully resist the temptation to eat it, you'll start believing more in your self-control abilities.

3. Eliminate another food or an entire group (for instance, all kinds of chocolate).

4. Introduce more vegetables in your diet. To make this change smaller, add just one piece of a vegetable per day.

5. Add some exercise in your routine. Even if it's just 30 minutes per week, it will suffice for now while you're building your self-efficacy.

…

10. Enjoy your new body.

By breaking your big goals into smaller, much more achievable steps, you'll ensure small wins that will help you develop more confidence in your abilities and make it easier to face bigger challenges.

Easy Success Isn't as Powerful as Blood, Sweat, and Tears Success

Your self-efficacy increases when you achieve successes, but it becomes much more firmly established when it's built on successes that required you to overcome obstacles through persistence.

If you only experience easy successes, you'll come to expect quick results with little to no effort. Consequently, you'll get easily discouraged when you face setbacks.

On the other hand, when you've already experienced successes after pushing through numerous obstacles, you'll be more resilient and capable of dealing with challenges[viii].

Arnold Schwarzenegger once said, "Strength does not come from winning. Your struggles develop your strengths. When you go through hardships and decide not to surrender, that is strength."

Mahatma Gandhi said something similar: "Strength does not come from physical capacity. It comes from an indomitable will."

Isn't it interesting how closely their words resemble the conclusions of scientific studies?

When you're struggling, remind yourself that it's your struggles which will make you a stronger, more resilient, and more successful person.

Failure, and When It Harms You the Most

Albert Bandura discovered that failure decreases self-efficacy. However, as I mentioned in the first chapter, people with a strong sense of self-efficacy don't approach failures in the same way as people with little belief in their abilities.

As failures are essential to achieve anything worthwhile in life, it's not a healthy approach to do everything in your power to avoid them. However, while you're working on developing your self-efficacy, it might be a good idea to minimize the risk of failures and focus on achieving small, safe goals.

When you experience a streak of successes, you'll become much more resilient and capable of dealing with failures in a positive, constructive way. Then, taking bigger risks won't be associated with a high risk of destroying your self-efficacy and sending you back to square one.

Failure Is Good

Even though acceptance of failure in society is steadily rising, many people still avoid setting big goals, as they associate the act of failing with a personal failure (*I failed, therefore I'm a failure*).

I've noticed this belief is not nearly as widespread in the entrepreneurial circles where failure is often celebrated. What's the difference between the general population and entrepreneurs?

Entrepreneurs consider failure a part of every achievement. As Richard Branson said[ix], "Failure and rejection are an inevitable part of business, and how you deal with them will ultimately affect your success. The ability to cope with and learn from failure and rejection can be practiced and honed along the way. Some people are better at it than others.

"We have had many great successes at Virgin, but we've also experienced a number of failures. Every time something hasn't worked out as we hoped it would, we have picked ourselves up, looked at what went wrong, and learned from our mistakes."

Therein lies the key to changing your beliefs about failure – it's just an opportunity to learn what doesn't work and do better next time.

Remind yourself of this concept each time you're afraid to fail. Surrounding yourself with people who approach failure in this way will also help you alter your beliefs.

If You Feel Extremely Uncomfortable with Failure, Try Rejection Therapy

Rejection therapy is a social game developed by Jason Comely, who for a year strived to become rejected every single day. The rules of his game are simple[x]:

1. You must be rejected by another person at least once, every single day.

2. Expecting more rules? Sorry to disappoint you. There's only one rule.

The only objective of the game is to get rejected. If your request is granted, you must ask for more – until you achieve the successful outcome, which is rejection.

Rejection therapy is not just a weird game created by a random person. It's an example of a psychotherapeutic technique called *flooding,* which was developed in 1967[xi].

It's still used by therapists to help patients overcome phobias. A patient is put into a situation where she faces her phobia at its worst. By facing the worst fear head on, the patient's fear gradually minimizes as she realizes it's not something to be afraid of.

Although flooding is not for everyone, as it's more traumatic than systematic desensitization (overcoming fear step by step), it can work pretty well to overcome your fear of failure. By facing rejection right away, you'll quickly notice the first results (weakened fear of rejection), which will help you become more at peace with failure.

Note I'm not a doctor, and you should never listen to self-help authors when your mental health is at stake. If you suffer from any mental health issues, speak with your doctor and consult a psychologist or a psychiatrist.

THE EXPERIENCE OF MASTERY: QUICK RECAP

1. Success breeds more success and builds your self-efficacy, while failure (when you believe it's bad for you) decreases it.

2. Ensure small wins to build your track record. Each small win will build more confidence in your abilities. If you have big goals that will take years to achieve, break them down into small bits.

3. The key to a strengthened sense of self-efficacy is not easy success; it's obstacles and perseverance that build your character, make you more resilient, and better equipped to handle setbacks.

4. Change your beliefs about failure – consider it a source of feedback, not a testament to your lack of abilities.

5. If you're afraid of failure, try rejection therapy. Make it a goal to get rejected by another person at least once, every single day. By exposing yourself to your worst fear, you will quickly become less

vulnerable to it (and ready to tackle bigger challenges).

Chapter 3: Social Modeling

Social modeling, or vicarious experience, which in simpler terms means watching and imitating other people, is the second factor influencing your self-efficacy.

It's not nearly as powerful as experiencing successes on your own, but it's still useful – especially when you have little confidence in your abilities and even small goals appear too big to achieve.

As with mastery experiences, watching others succeed increases your self-efficacy, while watching others fail decreases it.

However, self-efficacy built on social modeling alone is frail. If you try to do something after seeing someone succeed, but you fail, your self-efficacy will dramatically decrease – much more than if you were to fail after your previous small win.

The Behaviors of Your Friends Influence Your Own

An (in)famous Bobo doll experiment[xii] examined children's behavior after watching adults behave either aggressively or kindly towards a Bobo doll. The results showed that children in the group exposed to the aggressive behavior were more likely to act more aggressively toward the doll. The children who saw adults act kindly towards the doll were more likely to exhibit the same behavior.

Modeling works in exactly the same way for self-efficacy. When you watch people who constantly set the bar higher and higher, you also strive for more. When you watch people who fail, the belief in your abilities decreases and you want to remain in your safe bubble.

If your friends are likely to give up when faced with setbacks, it's likely you'll behave in the exact same way – after all, that's the model you've grown to know thanks to your friends.

If, on the other hand, they push through obstacles and keep going when you would have given up, it will inspire you to imitate their behavior when it's you who's struggling.

There are three important factors that can make social modeling even more powerful as an empowering tool:

1. Choosing the right model to imitate.

2. Joining a group of like-minded individuals.

3. Self-modeling.

We'll discuss these three concepts in the next three subchapters.

Choose the Right Model

The effect of social modeling is the strongest when you're watching a person who you see as similar to yourself[xiii]. In other words, you get more motivation from watching people slightly better than you succeed than from watching the pros.

It's much easier to relate to a person who has a similar level of skills. It will make you think that if she (a person similar to you) can do it, so can you.

Watching the pros, as inspiring as it is, results in a more detached experience. There's a wide gap in skills between them and you, so watching them succeed doesn't give you the same level of "I can do it, too" thoughts.

To give you an example from my personal life, reading biographies of successful entrepreneurs has never inspired me as much as watching fellow members of an online forum succeed. These were the guys I spoke with, who had the same exact thoughts and doubts as I did when starting out.

Seeing how they went from $0 per month to $100 per month to $1000, $2000, $5000 per month and beyond has had a much more powerful impact on me than reading about Richard Branson's newest bold venture (although it's inspiring to some extent, too).

Achieve Better Results with Public Accountability

Being a part of a group of people who share the same goal and are on a similar level works because of the Köhler effect[xiv] – people expend more effort in a group than they would if they had been working alone. Nobody wants to be the weakest link, so everyone works harder.

This effect is also stronger for women than men[xv].

Do you want to lose weight? Join online forums for regular people trying to lose weight. Interact with them, start your own progress thread and support others with a similar body type.

This simple practice will develop the confidence in your ability to lose weight to a much larger extent than watching motivational videos of fitness coaches who are difficult to relate to with their perfectly-sculpted bodies.

Do you want to learn a foreign language? Follow blogs of people who are just starting out with a new language, not polyglots. Polyglots have a powerful advantage over you – most languages share similar vocabulary, grammar rules, and other peculiarities that makes them easier to learn. It creates a knowledge gap between you and them, which makes it harder to relate to them.

Moreover, the more knowledge these experts have, the more difficult it is for them to relate to beginners (unless they have teaching experience).

Due to the curse of knowledge bias (you've forgotten what it's like not to have certain knowledge)[xvi], they have a hard time relating to the novice's situation.

No matter what goal you want to achieve, surround yourself with people on a similar level to inspire and motivate each other. This advice is especially important for people who want to lose weight, as having a fitness buddy is one of the most effective ways to push you harder when exercising[xvii].

Self-Modeling

Social modeling can help you develop more confidence in your abilities when you're watching yourself perform tasks successfully.

Consider recording yourself achieving a success or taking photos of your accomplishments. I also find it helpful to write about my successful experiences.

Let's imagine you're learning a new language. To improve your self-efficacy, you can record yourself while speaking on Skype with a language partner. You can agree beforehand what questions she will ask you and even the answers you'll give.

When you listen to yourself having a smooth conversation with a language partner (once you overcome the weird feeling of listening to your own voice), your self-efficacy will grow.

If you're working on a fitness-related goal, you can record yourself breaking your personal records. I taught myself how to correctly perform weightlifting exercises by recording myself practicing them and correcting my mistakes.

Once I learned how to do these exercises, I kept recording my workouts out of habit. Watching myself lift heavier and heavier weights built more confidence in my abilities.

You can combine self-modeling with participating in a group of like-minded individuals. If you successfully resisted the temptation to eat chocolate, write a post describing your success. If you sold your first product to a stranger, then brag on the forum for entrepreneurs. It will inspire people similar to you, while also building more confidence in your abilities.

SOCIAL MODELING: QUICK RECAP

1. Watching others succeed increases your self-efficacy, while watching others fail decreases it. However, self-efficacy can't be built on social modeling alone – achieving small wins is still the first thing you have to do to develop lasting self-efficacy.

2. It's easier to relate to people who are similar to you. You'll get a more powerful inspirational effect from watching a novice succeed than from observing the elite performers.

3. People expend more effort in a group than they would if they had been working alone. Participate in groups to motivate yourself to put in more effort and get better results.

4. Watching yourself succeed can be as effective as watching others succeed. Record yourself performing tasks successfully to increase your confidence.

Chapter 4: Social Persuasion and Psychological Responses

Verbal persuasion – encouragement or discouragement – is the third factor influencing your self-efficacy. It has an even weaker effect than social modeling.

Words of encouragement – whether they come from other people or from you – produce a short-term effect that can help you achieve a small win.

Words of discouragement, on the other hand, produce a short-term negative effect that can prevent you from pushing a little bit harder to achieve your goal. In the long term, negative input can undermine the confidence in your abilities.

Avoid Negativity – It's Stronger than Positivity

Discouragement has a more powerful negative impact on your behavior than the positive impact of encouragement because we pay more attention to the negative feedback[xviii].

For this reason, it's extremely important to avoid negative stimuli in your life, and do all in your power to avoid people who put others down. This can either happen naturally (you no longer invite them to meet and hope your relationship will gradually weaken) or more directly (you "break up" with them).

It's not always possible to cut ties with people who have a negative influence on you. Sometimes these people are members of our family or childhood friends, and there's no easy way to stop seeing them altogether.

In this case, focus on getting as much encouragement from other people as possible. While discouragement is stronger than encouragement, empowerment coming from many different sources will overpower discouraging words from one or two toxic individuals.

You Don't Need Others to Encourage Yourself

Positive self-talk can provide you with a short burst of motivation that will help you push through obstacles and reach the next level.

An example of positive self-talk is a simple "I can do it" when working out in the gym. When breaking my own personal records, I often remind myself of my previous sessions and tell myself I can do it again.

As discouragement is more powerful than encouragement, avoid letting negative thoughts affect your performance. If you feel something is outside your abilities, let the thought go and find a reason why you're capable of achieving it.

You won't lose anything by making yourself as ready as possible to tackle the challenge, while you'll lose a lot by letting negative self-talk instill a seed of doubt.

You can also use inspirational music as encouragement. Pick a song you like that has motivational lyrics and listen to it each time you're working on your goal.

That's what I did many years ago when I first started working on my fitness and set a goal to be able to perform 50 push-ups in a row. I listened to 2Pac's song "Hold On, Be Strong" while performing reps.

Corny, but it worked for me.

For Maximum Results, Find a Mentor

An experienced mentor (who knows how to relate to a novice) can greatly improve your self-efficacy in two ways – by giving you the right example (social modeling) and by encouraging you (social persuasion).

In today's era, it's extremely easy to find a mentor for virtually every area of your life. If you want to lose weight, you can hire a coach at your local gym. If you want to learn a foreign language, you can hire a native speaker of your target language as your private instructor. If you want to build a business, you can sign up for a seminar or boot camp for entrepreneurs.

Mentorship doesn't always have to be costly. Think outside the box when looking for a teacher. You can exchange skills (language instruction in English in exchange for language instruction in Spanish), find people who are just starting out and have low rates, or contribute to online forums to get noticed by a mentor.

Psychological Responses, the Least Important Source of Self-Efficacy

Physiological factors like shaking, aches and pains, fatigue, fear, nausea, and butterflies in the stomach have the weakest influence on your self-efficacy.

Yet, for a person with a weak sense of self-efficacy, they add another barrier that will make a person doubt in her abilities and affect her performance.

What's important to note is that it's not the reaction alone that makes you doubt your abilities – it's how you interpret it.

People with a strong sense of self-efficacy don't associate these psychological responses with their lack of ability – they interpret them as normal reactions before performing a task. People with low self-efficacy, on the other hand, interpret these reactions as a sign of their weak abilities, thus increasing their self-doubt.

If these symptoms make you doubt in your abilities, it's time to change your beliefs about physiological reactions related to stress.

Each time you experience shaking, butterflies in your stomach or fear, consider it a normal reaction of your body's heightened awareness. Think that it's excitement, not anxiety.

Even professional speakers get jittery before a presentation, and it has nothing to do with their ability to perform on stage. Try rejection therapy mentioned in the second chapter as a way to get used to these symptoms.

You can also practice stress management techniques like meditation or envision yourself performing the task successfully. I spend more time covering these two techniques in my books *How to Build Self-Discipline: Resist Temptations and Reach*

Your Long-Term Goals and *Grit: How to Keep Going When You Want to Give Up*.

By learning how to better control anxiety, you'll reduce the influence of these symptoms on your self-efficacy. However, putting the most focus on the first two factors that influence your self-efficacy will lead to better results than bothering yourself with the little details.

SOCIAL PERSUASION AND PSYCHOLOGICAL RESPONSES: QUICK RECAP

1. Social persuasion in the form of encouraging or discouraging words has a weaker effect than mastery experiences and social modeling. However, frequent encouragement can still build your self-efficacy, while frequent discouragement can ruin your confidence.

2. Discouragement is more effective at decreasing your self-efficacy than encouragement is at increasing it. It's paramount to do all in your power to avoid negative people, as it's even more important than surrounding yourself with people who will empower you.

3. You don't need others to benefit from social persuasion. Positive self-talk (saying to yourself things like "I can do it," "I'm pretty good at this") will give you a short burst of motivation that can help you achieve small wins that will add up to big wins. Listening to motivational music can also work.

4. Psychological responses to stress like shaking, aches and pains, fatigue, fear, nausea, butterflies in the stomach can affect your self-efficacy if you believe that these signs are associated with your inability to perform.

5. The first step to reduce the influence of psychological responses on your self-efficacy is to instill in yourself a belief that even the pros experience the same signs of distress as you do. Since these reactions are common even among highly-skilled people, they don't mean your abilities are lacking.

6. Practice stress management techniques to decrease the symptoms of stress. Put yourself in uncomfortable situations to get used to these reactions. However, keep in mind that your time will be better spent on achieving small wins and imitating others than trying to reduce the symptoms of anxiety.

Chapter 5: Five Rules to Develop a Strong Sense of Self-Efficacy

While there are dozens of techniques to develop more self-efficacy, there are only five fundamental rules that will provide you with more results than the rest of the little tricks combined.

No matter how much you remember from other chapters, this chapter alone will still be enough to benefit from this book and develop more confidence in your abilities. The key, as with everything else, is to focus on the process, not the event. Self-efficacy can't be built overnight, but these small blocks add up quickly to a strong foundation.

Set Goals Slightly Above Your Ability

There are three personal zones of achievement – comfort zone, stretch zone and panic zone. Look at the image below:

PANIC ZONE

STRETCH ZONE

COMFORT ZONE

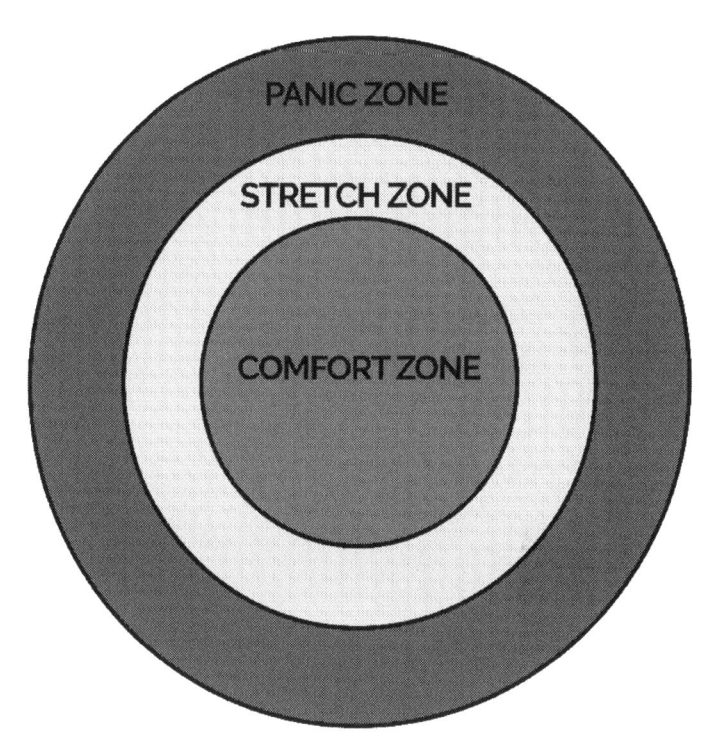

Comfort zone encompasses all of the things you're familiar with. These are all the things that are comfortable and easy to do – skills you already possess, spending time with people you know, learning about concepts with which you're familiar.

Panic zone consists of all the things outside your ability – trying them will lead to panic and decreased self-efficacy. These are things way outside your abilities, like public speaking in front of a huge audience while you can't present in front of a few people.

Stretch zone is where you want to be – it contains all of the things that are challenging, yet possible to achieve with your current level of abilities. Things that belong to this zone are within your reach, but make you feel uncomfortable – e.g., chatting up a random stranger while you find it challenging to ask for the time.

By setting goals slightly above your ability, you will gradually improve the confidence in your abilities. Each small win will build on top of the previous one, combining into a big achievement that will do wonders to your self-efficacy.

The question of how to stretch your comfort zone depends on your personality. Some people prefer small steps, venturing just a few steps outside their comfort zone. Others (like me) prefer the more extreme approach and trying things bordering the panic zone.

The former approach is slower, but less traumatic, and with a lower risk of failure. The latter approach is perfect for people who are impatient, and are okay with the increased chance of failure.

Try both of these approaches and see which one works better for you.

To give you an example, let's say you possess weak self-efficacy in regards to waking up early. You don't believe you can wake up earlier than, say, 10 AM, but you'd like to change it.

The first approach would be to slowly start waking up earlier and earlier – 9:55, 9:50, 9:45, and so on, so that in less than two weeks you'll wake up an hour sooner. This will develop the belief that since you were capable of constantly waking up 5 minutes sooner, you can keep doing it until you achieve your target hour.

The second approach (the one I prefer and used to change my daily schedule) is to set your target hour and wake up right away this early. For instance, if your goal is to start waking up at 6 AM, you set your alarm for 6 AM.

There's a higher risk of failure (after all, it's not that easy to wake up four hours earlier than usual), but if you succeed the first day, the sense of achievement will help you wake up early again the next day.

A shy person who wants to become more confident has two options, too. The first way is to focus on small challenges and increase the difficulty gradually (ask strangers for the time, for the directions, chat up a clerk in the store, talk with a random stranger). The second way is to pick the biggest challenge (but not so big that it leads to paralyzing panic) and face it head on (public speaking, approaching a random stranger, etc.).

Break Goals into Smaller Pieces and Simplify

People with low self-efficacy believe that tasks are harder than they actually are. Consequently, they don't plan properly (after all, what's the difference if you think these tasks are too hard?). It's a vicious cycle – you don't plan your tasks because you think they're hard, and these tasks are hard exactly because you don't plan them.

It's easy to get overwhelmed, especially when you don't believe in your abilities. Building a business feels like building a medieval castle brick by brick with your bare hands. Shyness feels like a lifetime sentence without parole. It feels as if it's going to take decades to master a foreign language.

According to the 80/20 rule, 80% of the results come from 20% of the efforts. Breaking your goal into small bite-sized pieces that provide the biggest benefits is the key to develop more confidence in your skills.

Let's say you want to learn how to speak a foreign language. There are many aspects of a language – hundreds of grammar rules, thousands of new words, new pronunciation and intonation rules, sometimes a new alphabet or characters.

However, do you really need to master all of these things right away? If your goal to learn a foreign language is to communicate with native speakers, all you need to focus on is the ability to speak with them. Writing isn't important now.

Neither is grammar or imitating the sounds of native speakers perfectly.

Let's break it further, as "the ability to speak with native speakers" is still too vague and can provoke self-doubt. What's the key thing you need to master? Let's say it's a hundred or so basic sentences, questions and statements. Suddenly the huge goal doesn't seem so overwhelming – in a week or two, you can develop an ability to hold a simple conversation in another language.

Ask yourself how you can break your own goal into smaller parts. Consider how you can cut away the unessential to reach the core of the issue. The more manageable you make your goal, the more confident you'll be in your abilities to reach it.

A simple way to help you break your goals into smaller parts is mind mapping. I use free software called XMind to break huge concepts into smaller, easy-to-digest key aspects, which I further break into the most fundamental ones.

Focus on the Big Picture

As American author, speaker and pastor John C. Maxwell said, "You cannot overestimate the unimportance of practically everything."

Don't waste your time (and energy) worrying about the little details.

People with a strong sense of self-efficacy take a wider view of their goal in order to create the best plan. It starts with breaking it into smaller parts, but what's even more important is looking for the root of the problem.

A study on experts and novices[xix] shows that novices get stuck thinking about the surface of the problem, while experts look deeper and concentrate on the underlying principles. It's not the tactics that are important – it's the strategy.

Gary Keller describes this approach perfectly in his book *The ONE Thing: The Surprisingly Simple Truth Behind Extraordinary Results*[xx] by asking himself, "What's the one thing I can do, such that by doing it everything else is easier or unnecessary?"

A person who doesn't believe in her abilities will start with an unfocused plan. Consequently, she'll have a hard time working on her goal.

On the other hand, a person with high self-efficacy will first spend time identifying just one thing – a priority that will render everything else unnecessary – and only then start working on her goal.

Reframe Obstacles

Cognitive reframing is a psychological technique of identifying and replacing negative beliefs, attitudes and ideas with the positive ones. One of the most important characteristics of people with high self-efficacy is that obstacles motivate them to keep going. Their underlying belief is that each obstacle they overcome is a step closer to success.

If you want to improve the confidence in your abilities, changing how you think about obstacles is key. People with low self-efficacy consider setbacks the proof that they should give up. Their thinking usually goes something along the lines of, "Damn, another obstacle. This is too hard. Life is telling me I can't achieve this goal."

Restructuring how you think about obstacles is a process that starts with self-awareness. Each time you find yourself discouraged and ready to give up when faced with an obstacle, remind yourself that they are there for a reason.

As American professor Randy Pausch said, "The brick walls are there for a reason. The brick walls are not there to keep us out. The brick walls are there to give us a chance to show how badly we want something. Because the brick walls are there to stop the people who don't want it badly enough. They're there to stop the other people.[xxi]"

By being aware of your thoughts and actively trying to replace them with the opposite thought, you will slowly reduce the power of this belief on your self-efficacy. Soon, you'll stop thinking of obstacles as the reason why you need to give up, and you'll start thinking of them as the reason why you need to keep going.

Below are a couple of examples of reframing:

Original thought: A native speaker couldn't understand when I told him about my family. I'll never learn a foreign language.

Reframed thought: A native speaker couldn't understand when I told him about my family. Now I know I need to spend more time learning vocabulary related to family.

Original thought: I tried speaking with a cute girl and she brushed me off. I'm so awkward there's no way I'll ever become confident.

Reframed thought: I tried speaking with a cute girl and she brushed me off. It helped me deal with rejection and gave me ideas how to improve my conversational skills.

Original thought: I lost all money I invested in my business that never took off. I better focus on my day job, as I will never succeed as an entrepreneur.

Reframed thought: I lost all money I invested in my business that never took off. I learned what doesn't work and will apply these lessons when starting my next venture that's bound to be more successful.

Take Control over Your Life

People with high self-efficacy believe that their own actions and decisions shape their lives, while individuals who lack a belief in their abilities may see their lives as outside their control.

In psychology, this concept is called *locus of control*[xxii] – the extent to which you believe you can control events that affect you.

Changing your worldview is fundamental if you'd like to develop self-efficacy. There's no shortcut to change it overnight, though. Your personal experiences and your interpretation of them has deeply ingrained your beliefs about the locus of control.

For one person (with high self-efficacy), losing money on a new business venture is the result of her wrong hiring decisions, bad business idea, or not enough capital. Another person (with low self-efficacy) will blame the economy (even though there are always businesses that thrive during the crisis).

You can change your beliefs about control in a similar way to changing your beliefs about obstacles.

Each time you blame something or someone else for your failure, think of the reasons why it could have been the result of your actions and decisions.

Taking responsibility for your actions is difficult at first, but once you learn how to acknowledge your mistakes, you'll be able to improve your performance. Moreover, shifting your locus of control from external to internal factors will reduce your stress levels[xxiii] – which, in turn, will also improve your performance.

To give you an example, one of my most notable failures was starting a software business. Just a few months after I invested a considerable amount of money in it, I decided to call it quits.

It would be easy to say it failed because the world was against me, because the economy made my potential clients poor or something like that. But that wasn't the case, and never is. The business failed because *I* shouldn't have started it in the first place. It failed to grow because it was *me* who sabotaged it. Everything was in my control, and it was my control that made this business fail.

As strange as it may sound, I find it a reassuring thought to know that it failed because of me. For a simple reason – I knew exactly what caused its demise, and I'll do better next time. If it was something outside my control, I couldn't learn anything from this failure. And that's precisely the opposite of how to build self-efficacy.

FIVE RULES TO DEVELOP A STRONG SENSE OF SELF-EFFICACY: QUICK RECAP

1. Set goals slightly above your ability to gradually increase your self-efficacy. There are two approaches you can take – do things that lay just a few steps outside your comfort zone (and wait for the results longer, with a lower chance of failure) or try something more difficult that borders your panic zone (where growth is extremely difficult).

2. Break goals into smaller pieces and simplify your tasks. The more you cut away, the less overwhelming your goal will appear, which will help you overcome the disbelief in your abilities. Remember about the 80/20 rule that says that 80% of the results come from the 20% of the efforts.

3. Look deeper than the surface. Find the underlying principles that will help you achieve success instead of looking for the little secrets (there are none).

4. Change how you think about obstacles. Start with self-awareness and monitor your thoughts. When

you catch yourself thinking why the setbacks prove that you should give up, come up with the opposite thought – why they mean you should keep going.

5. People with high self-efficacy believe that it's their actions and decisions that affect their life. If you want to develop more confidence in your abilities, you need to change your worldview and accept the responsibility for your own life. No amount of blaming something or someone else will help you make your life better.

Epilogue

In the five chapters of this book, we covered the most fundamental knowledge that will help you develop more confidence in your abilities. Yet, let's be clear: reading this book alone won't make any lasting changes in your life.

If you don't actively work on developing your self-efficacy, making any kind of changes in your life will be an extremely difficult ordeal.

If you're starting with low self-efficacy, your first step is to achieve some small wins. Pick an area of your life you'd like to work on, and ask yourself what little changes you can introduce in your life. This will help you build more confidence in your abilities.

Once you enjoy several small wins, it's time to put into use other concepts from this book. Most notably:

1. Surround yourself with the right, successful people and model your behavior after them. Besides your own experiences, there's nothing that has a more

powerful impact on your self-efficacy than watching others succeed.

2. Reduce the time spent with negative people who discourage you. Or if possible, avoid them altogether. Discouragement has a destructive effect on your self-efficacy – especially if you don't possess a strong sense of it.

3. Come up with your own strategies to deal with stress. Better yet – change your attitude toward stress and stop associating it with a lack of abilities. Even the pros get butterflies in their stomachs before an important keynote.

4. Take control over your life, break your goals (that should be slightly above your abilities) into smaller pieces and focus on the big picture. It's not the little details that make the difference – it's the focus on the most important things.

5. A strong sense of self-efficacy is about the deep belief in your abilities, not about cockiness or your self-esteem alone. Focus on achieving the mastery, but stay humble and open to new ideas just like a novice.

This book is by no means the only thing you need to read to achieve your goals. Success is a process, not an event. However, I strived to cover the most important aspects of self-efficacy and provide you with actionable tips to improve your life in as little time as possible.

If you feel inspired, and more importantly, if you're going to close this book and work on your goals with a newfound understanding of your personal beliefs, my goal has been achieved.

Download another Book for Free

I want to thank you for buying my book and offer you another book (almost two times longer than this book), *Grit: How to Keep Going When You Want to Give Up,* completely free.

Visit the link below to receive it:

http://www.profoundselfimprovement.com/selfefficacy

In *Grit*, I'll share with you how exactly to stick to your goals according to peak performers and science.

In addition to getting *Grit*, you'll also have an opportunity to get my new books for free, enter giveaways and receive other valuable emails from me.

Again, here's the link to sign up and get the book:

http://www.profoundselfimprovement.com/selfefficacy

Could You Help?

I'd love to hear your opinion about my book. In the world of book publishing, there are few things more valuable than honest reviews from a wide variety of readers.

Your review will help other readers find out whether my book is for them. It will also help me reach more readers by increasing the visibility of my book.

About Martin Meadows

Martin Meadows is the pen name of a bestselling author who has dedicated his life to personal growth. He constantly reinvents himself by making drastic changes in his life.

Over the years, he has regularly fasted for over 40 hours, taught himself two foreign languages, lost over 30 pounds in 12 weeks, ran several businesses in various industries, took ice-cold showers and baths, lived on a small tropical island in a foreign country for several months, and wrote a 400-page long novel's worth of short stories in one month.

Yet, self-torture is not his passion. Martin likes to test his boundaries to discover how far his comfort zone goes.

His findings (based both on his personal experience and scientific studies) help him improve his life. If you're interested in pushing your limits and learning how to become the best version of yourself, you'll love Martin's works.

You can read his books here:

http://www.amazon.com/author/martinmeadows.

© Copyright 2015 by Meadows Publishing. All rights reserved.

Reproduction in whole or in part of this publication without express written consent is strictly prohibited. The author greatly appreciates you taking the time to read his work. Please consider leaving a review wherever you bought the book, or telling your friends about it, to help us spread the word. Thank you for supporting our work.

Efforts have been made to ensure that the information in this book is accurate and complete. However, the author and the publisher do not warrant the accuracy of the information, text and graphics contained within the book due to the rapidly changing nature of science, research, known and unknown facts and the Internet. The author and the publisher do not hold any responsibility for errors, omissions or contrary interpretation of the subject matter herein. This book is presented solely for motivational and informational purposes only.

---

[i] Bandura A. (1994) *Self-efficacy*. In V. S. Ramachaudran (Ed.), *Encyclopedia of human behavior*, New York: Academic Press, pp. 71–81.

[ii] McNatt D. B., Judge T. A. "Boundary Conditions of the Galatea Effect: A Field Experiment and Constructive Replication." *Academy of Management Journal* 2004; 47 (4): 550–565.

[iii] Luszczynska A., Schwarzer R. (2005). *Social cognitive theory*. In M. Conner & P. Norman (Eds.), *Predicting health behaviour* (2nd edition revisited). Buckingham, England: Open University Press, pp. 127–169.

[iv] Weinberg R. S., Gould D., (2007) *Foundation of Sport and Exercise Psychology* (4th edition). Champaign, IL: Human Kinetics, p. 422.

[v] Suzuki S. *Zen Mind, Beginner's Mind*.

[vi] Diamandis P. H., Kotler S., *Bold: How to Go Big, Create Wealth and Impact the World*, 2015.

[vii] For more information about keystone habits, read my book *How to Build Self-Discipline: Resist Temptations and Reach Your Long-Term Goals*.

[viii] Bandura A. (1997) *Self-efficacy: The exercise of control*. New York: Freeman.

[ix] http://www.forbes.com/sites/alisoncoleman/2015/03/15/why-richard-branson-thinks-failure-should-be-an-option-for-all-entrepreneurs/, Web. March 16th, 2015.

[x] http://rejectiontherapy.com/rules/, Web. March 16th, 2015.

[xi] Leitenberg H. (1990). *Handbook of Social and Evaluation Anxiety*. Springer, pp. 300–302.

[xii] Bandura A., Ross D., Ross S. A. "Imitation of film-mediated aggressive models." *The Journal of Abnormal and Social Psychology* 1963; 66 (1): 3–11.

[xiii] Brown I., Inouye D. K. "Learned helplessness through modeling: The role of perceived similarity in competence." *Journal of Personality and Social Psychology* 1978, 36 (8): 900–908. See also: Bandura, A. (1981). *Self-referent thought: A development analysis of self-efficacy*. In J. H. Flavell & L. Ross (Eds.), *Social cognitive development: Frontiers and possible futures* (pp. 200–239). Cambridge, England: Cambridge University Press.

[xiv] Hertel G., Kerr N. L., Messé L. A. "Motivation gains in performance groups: paradigmatic and theoretical developments on the Köhler effect." *Journal of Personality and Social Psychology* 2000; 79 (4): 580–601.

[xv] Weber B., Hertel G. "Motivation gains of inferior group members: a meta-analytical review." *Journal of Personality and Social Psychology* 2007; 93 (6): 973–993.

[xvi] Camerer C., Loewenstein G., Weber M. "The curse of knowledge in economic settings: An experimental analysis." *Journal of Political Economy* 1989; 97: 1232–1254.

[xvii] Brandon C. I., Scorniaenchi J., Kerr N. L., Eisenmann J. C., Feltz D. L. "Aerobic Exercise Is Promoted when Individual Performance Affects the Group: A Test of the Köhler Motivation Gain Effect." *Annals of Behavioral Medicine* 2012; 44 (2): 151–159.

[xviii] Baumeister R.F., Bratslavsky E., Finkenauer C., Vohs K. D. "Bad is stronger than good." *Review of General Psychology* 2001; 5: 323–370.

[xix] Chi M. T. H., Feltovich P. J., Glaser R. "Categorization and Representation of Physics Problems by Experts and Novices." *Cognitive Science* 1981; 5 (2): 121–152.

[xx] Keller G., Papasan J., *The ONE Thing: The Surprisingly Simple Truth Behind Extraordinary Results*.

[xxi] Pausch R. *The Last Lecture*.

[xxii] Rotter J. B. "Generalized expectancies for internal versus external control of reinforcement." *Psychological Monographs: General & Applied* 1966, 80 (1): 1–28.

[xxiii] Roddenberry A., Renk K. "Locus of Control and Self-Efficacy: Potential Mediators of Stress, Illness, and Utilization of Health Services in College Students." *Child Psychiatry & Human Development* 2010; 41 (4): 353–370.

Printed in Great Britain
by Amazon